The Nobel Lecture
on Literature

Aleksandr I. Solzhenitsyn

THE NOBEL LECTURE
ON LITERATURE

*Translated from the Russian
by Thomas P. Whitney*

HARPER & ROW, PUBLISHERS
NEW YORK, EVANSTON, SAN FRANCISCO, LONDON

1817

This translation, in slightly different form, appeared in the
New York Times on September 30, 1972, and October 7, 1972.

FIRST EDITION

STANDARD BOOK NUMBER: 06-013943-9

LIBRARY OF CONGRESS CATALOG CARD NUMBER: 72-9890

Designed by Peter Mollman

The Nobel Lecture
on Literature

1

LIKE THAT BEWILDERED savage who has picked up a strange object . . . perhaps something thrown up by the sea, perhaps disinterred from the sands or dropped from the heavens . . . an object intricate in its convolutions, which shines first with a dull glow and then with a bright shaft of light . . . who keeps turning it over and over in his hands in an effort to find some way of putting it to use, seeking some humble function for it, which is within his limited grasp, never conceiving of a higher purpose . . .

So we, too, holding art in our hands, vaingloriously considering ourselves to be its master, undertake brazenly to give it direction, to renovate it, to reform it, to issue manifestoes about it, to sell it for money. We use it to play up to those who possess power. We employ it at times for amusement—even in music hall songs and night clubs—and also, at times, grabbing hold of it however we can, for transient and limited political and social needs. But art is not desecrated by our carryings-on. It does not lose sight of its own origins because of them. And each time and in each mode of use it sheds on us a portion of its secret inner light.

But can we embrace *all* that light? Who is there so bold as to proclaim that he has DEFINED art? That he has enumerated all its facets? Yet perhaps in ages past someone did comprehend and define it for us, but we grew impatient: we listened in passing and paid no heed and discarded it immediately in our eternal haste to replace even the very best with something else just because it is new! And then later on, when what is old is restated, we forget that we heard it before.

One artist imagines himself the creator of an independent spiritual world and takes on his shoulders the act of creating that world and its population, assuming total responsibility for it—but he stumbles and breaks down because there is no mortal genius capable of bearing such a load; just like man, who once declared himself the center of all existence but was incapable of creating a balanced spiritual system. And then, when failure occurs, it is all blamed on the eternal disharmony of the world, on the complexity of the shattered contemporary soul, or on the stupidity of the public.

Another artist realizes that there is a supreme force above him and works away gladly as a small apprentice beneath God's heaven, even though his responsibility for everything he writes or draws and for the souls which perceive it is all the more strict. But still: it was not he who created this world, nor is it he who provides it with direction, and he has no doubts of its foundations. The artist is only given to sense more keenly than others the harmony of the world and all the beauty and savagery of man's contribution to it—and to communicate this poignantly to people. And even in the midst of failure and down at the lowest depths of existence—in poverty, prison, illness—the sensation of a stable harmony will never leave him.

However, all the irrationality of art, its blinding twists and turns, its unpredictable discoveries, its soul-shaking impact on people are too magical to be contained within the world-outlook of an artist, in his conception or in the work of his unworthy fingers.

Archaeologists have not yet discovered any stage of human existence without art. Even in the half-light before the dawn of humanity we received this gift from Hands we did not manage to discern. Nor have we managed to ask: Why was this gift given us and what are we to do with it?

And all those prophets who are predicting that art is disintegrating, that it has used up all its forms, that it is dying, are mistaken. We are the ones who shall die. And art will remain. The question is whether before we perish we shall understand all its aspects and all its ends.

Not all can be given names. Some of them go beyond words. Art opens even the chilled, darkened heart to high spiritual experience. Through the instrumentality of art we are sometimes sent—vaguely, briefly—insights which logical processes of thought cannot attain.

Like the tiny mirror of the fairy tale: you look into it and you see—not yourself—but for one fleeting moment the Unattainable to which you cannot leap or fly. And the heart aches. . . .

2

DOSTOYEVSKY ONCE LET DROP the enigmatic phrase: "Beauty will save the world." What does this mean? For a long time it used to seem to me that this was a mere phrase. Just how could such a thing be possible? When had it ever happened in the blood-thirsty course of history that beauty had saved anyone from anything? Beauty had provided embellishment certainly, given uplift—but whom had it ever saved?

However, there is a special quality in the essence of beauty, a special quality in the status of art: the conviction carried by a genuine work of art is absolutely indisputable and tames even the strongly opposed heart. One can construct a political speech, an assertive journalistic polemic, a program for organizing society, a philosophical system, so that in appearance it is smooth, well structured, and yet it is built upon a mistake, a lie; and the hidden element, the distortion, will not immediately become visible. And a speech, or a journalistic essay, or a program in rebuttal, or a different philosophical structure can be counterposed to the first—and it will seem just as well constructed and as smooth, and everything will seem to fit. And therefore one has faith in them—yet one has no faith.

It is in vain to affirm that which the heart does not confirm.

In contrast, a work of art bears within itself its own confirmation: concepts which are manufactured out of whole cloth or overstrained will not stand up to being tested in images, will somehow fall apart and turn out to be sickly and pallid and convincing to no one. Works steeped in truth and presenting it to us vividly alive will take hold of us, will attract us to themselves with great power—and no one, ever, even in a later age, will presume to negate them. And so perhaps that old trinity of Truth, Good, and Beauty is not just the formal outworn formula it used to seem to us during our heady, materialistic youth. If the crests of these three trees

6

join together, as the investigators and explorers used to affirm, and if the too obvious, too straight branches of Truth and Good are crushed or amputated and cannot reach the light—yet perhaps the whimsical, unpredictable, unexpected branches of Beauty will make their way through and soar up TO THAT VERY PLACE and in this way perform the work of all three.

And in that case it was not a slip of the tongue for Dostoyevsky to say that "Beauty will save the world," but a prophecy. After all *he* was given the gift of seeing much, he was extraordinarily illumined.

And consequently perhaps art, literature, can in actual fact help the world of today.

That little which I have managed to discern over the years I shall try to set forth here today.

3

I HAVE CLIMBED my way up to this lectern from which the Nobel Lecture is read, a lectern not granted to every writer and once only in a lifetime, not just up three or four specially erected steps but hundreds and even thousands of them—unyielding, steep, frozen, out of the dark and the cold where I was fated to survive and where others, who possessed perhaps greater talent and were stronger than I, perished. I met only a few among them in the Gulag Archipelago scattered over a wide-spread multitude of islands. And beneath the mill-stone of police surveillance and mistrust I did not speak face to face with all those who were there either. Of some I only heard at second hand and about others I only guessed. Those who fell into that abyss who already had made a name in literat̶ ̶a̶re at least known to us—but how many wer̶ unknown, had never been published! And so very few, almost no one, managed to survive and return. A whole national literature remained behind, buried not only without coffins and graves, but even without underwear, naked except for an identification tag on the toe. Russian literature never ceased for one moment! Yet from outside it seemed a desert. Where a thick forest might have grown there remained, after all the timbering, only two or three trees which had missed being cut down.

And today how am I, accompanied as I am by the spirits of those who perished, my head bowed as I let pass before me up to this lectern others who were earlier worthy of it, how am I here today supposed to divine and express that which *they* would have wished to say?

This duty has long weighed upon me, and I have understood it. In the words of Vladimir Soloviev:

> In chains, too, we must close the circle
> Which the gods have drawn for us.

In exhausting camp marches, rows of lanterns lighting the columns of prisoners in the darkness of subzero nights, more than once we felt in our throats what we would have liked to shout out to the whole world, if only the world could have heard some spokesman from among us. At that time it seemed so very, very clear that all our lucky envoy had to do was to raise an outcry and instantly the whole world would respond. Our entire outlook, in terms of both material objects and emotional actions and reactions, was precisely defined. And we sensed no lack of balance in the indivisible world. Those thoughts did not come from books and had not been taken over for the sake of harmony and good order: they had been formulated in prison cells and around timber-camp bonfires in conversations with people long since dead who had emerged tried and true from that life, who had matured in that existence.

When the external pressure lessened, our outlook and my own outlook broadened, and gradually, if only through a peephole, the "whole world" could be seen and discerned. And, surprisingly for us, that "whole world" turned out to be something quite different from what we had expected it to be. It did not live by what we had expected. It was proceeding to a destination we had not anticipated. When it came to a swampy bog, it exclaimed:

"What a divine and lovely lawn!" When it encountered stocks made of concrete that were going to be placed around the necks of prisoners, it exclaimed: "What a lovely necklace!" And where unquenchable tears poured forth for some, others danced to lighthearted music.

So how has this come about? Whence has this abyss arisen? Were we all unfeeling? Or was the world unfeeling? Or was it due to the difference in languages? How does it happen that people are unable to understand each other's plain speech? Words resound and flow away like water—without taste, or color, or odor. Without a trace.

To the extent that I have come to understand this, the content, meaning, and tone of my possible speech here have changed over and over again with the years . . . the speech that I am delivering today.

It is by now very little like that speech which I first conceived in the subzero cold of the camp nights.

4

From time immemorial the human being has been structured in such a way that his world-outlook, at least when not induced by hypnosis, his motivations and scale of values, his actions and intentions are determined by his own personal and group life-experience. As the Russian proverb says:

"Believe not your own brother—believe, instead, your own blind eye."

This is the healthiest foundation for understanding one's surroundings and for one's behavior in them. And through all those long ages when our world was so mysteriously, remotely separated, before it was crisscrossed by unifying lines of communication, before it was transformed into a united and tremulously beating clump, people were guided unerringly by their own life-experience in their own limited locality, in their own community, in their own society, and in the end in their own national territory. In those times it was possible for individual human eyes to perceive and accept a certain common scale of values: what was recognized as being average, as being improbable or unlikely, as being cruel, harsh; what was regarded as being beyond all bounds of evil-doing; what was honorable; what was deceit. And even though widely scattered peoples lived in different ways, even though their scale of social values might be astonishingly at variance, just as, in fact, their systems of weights and measures were at variance, these differences surprised only infrequent travelers, and were collected for publication in various journals as curiosities which held no danger for a still un-united humanity.

But then, in our most recent decades, humanity has imperceptibly and suddenly become united— hopefully united and dangerously united. So that a concussion or an infection in one part is almost instantly transmitted to other parts, which sometimes have no immunity at all against it. Humanity has become united—but not as a community or even a nation used to be united in a state of stability: not as a result of gradual life-experience, not through the sight of one's own EYE which in the proverb was jocularly called blind, not even through one's own native and comprehensible language—but instead, in spite of and across all the obstacles and barriers, by the international radio and press. Down upon us rolls a tidal wave of events. In one brief moment half the world learns of their appearance, but the standard for measuring these events, for evaluating them—in accordance with the laws of parts of the world unknown to us—is not and cannot be carried by the ether or in newspaper columns: these standards have been established and accepted for too long and in too special a way in the isolated lives of separate countries and societies. They cannot be communicated instantaneously. And in different regions different, particular, hard-won scales of values are applied—and judgment is delivered uncompromisingly, boldly, solely on the basis of one's own particular scale of values and without regard for the scales of others.

Though there are not necessarily a multitude of such scales in the world, there are at least several: a scale of values to be applied to events close at hand and a scale to be applied to events far distant; a scale to be applied to old and developed societies and a different one for those which are young and undeveloped; one scale for societies that are well-off and quite another for those that are not. The dividing lines on the different scales are so startlingly different from each other, so varied in color, that they hurt the eyes, and so as not to feel the pain we brush aside those scales of values which are not our own as if they were madness, as if they would lead us into delusion—and we judge the world self-confidently on the basis of our own domestic scale of values. As a result, the things which seem to us to be larger, more painful, more insufferable are not those that really are so—but those that are closest to us. Everything distant from us, everything that does not threaten to roll across the threshold of our home this very day, is seen by us with all its moans, groans, stifled screams, destroyed lives —even when millions of victims are involved— as being by and large endurable and existing within tolerable dimensions.

On one side of the scale, amid persecutions which yielded nothing to those of ancient Rome, hundreds of thousands of silent, unheard Christians sacrificed their lives for their faith in God. And in the other hemisphere a certain madman (no doubt not the only one either) dashed across the ocean TO FREE us from religion with a blow of steel directed at the pontiff! On the basis of his own scale he undertook to make this decision for all the rest of us!

What on one scale of values seems from a distance to be an enviable and blessed freedom, on another scale, close up, is perceived as a regrettable compulsion obliging us to overturn buses. What in one region would be dreamed of as a totally improbable prosperity and well-being, in another arouses outrage as savage exploitation that calls for an immediate strike. Various scales exist for natural catastrophes: a flood which takes two hundred thousand lives seems a less important event than some accident in our own town. There are different scales for insults to persons: in some places even an ironic smirk or a gesture of dismissal is a humiliation, while in others cruel beatings are regarded as being just as forgivable as a bad joke. There are different scales for punishments and for evil deeds. According to one scale, a month of arrest, or of exile to a rural area, or confinement in a "punishment cell" where the prisoner is fed on white rolls and milk, shakes the imagination and floods the columns of the newspapers with rage. And on another scale, prison terms of twenty-five years and punishment cells with ice on the walls in which prisoners are forced to undress down to their underwear, and insane asylums for healthy people, and shots fired by border guards into innumerable unreasonable people who are always for some strange reason trying to escape—all these things are quite ordinary and excusable. And the heart is particularly at ease with that exotic land about which in fact nothing at all is really known, whence no news at all of actual events reaches our ears, except the tardy and trivial conjectures of a few correspondents.

And for this dichotomy, for this dumfounded incapacity to grasp someone else's far-off grief, one cannot reproach human eyesight: that is the way the human being is. But for humanity as a whole, packed into one single clump, such mutual lack of understanding carries the threat of a quick and stormy death. Given the existence of six, or four, or even two scales of values, there can be no united world, no united humanity: we will be torn apart by this difference in rhythm, this difference in oscillation. We will not survive on one Earth, just as no man can survive with two hearts.

5

BUT JUST WHO is going to coordinate these scales of values, and how is it to be done? Who is going to create for all humanity one single unitary system of evaluation—for evil deeds and good deeds, for what is intolerable and what is tolerable, and where the boundary between them lies today? Who is going to clarify for all humanity what is genuinely heinous and unbearable and what merely scrapes our skin because of its proximity—and thereby direct our wrath against what is really the most terrible, not against what is merely the nearest? Just who is there who might be able to communicate such an understanding through the barriers of personal human experience? Who is there who might possibly be able to instill in the bigoted, narrow, stubborn human essence the grief and joy of those faraway others, the perception of a range of facts and delusions never personally experienced?

In this area propaganda, and coercion, and scientific proofs are all powerless. But fortunately there does exist in the world a means to this end! It is art. It is literature.

A miracle is within its power: to overcome the human being's liability of learning only from personal experience, so that the experience of others bypasses him with no effect. From human being to human being, filling up their brief time on earth, art communicates entire the freight of someone else's long life-experience, with all its burdens, colors, juices, recreating the experience endured by another human being in the flesh—permitting it to be absorbed and made one's own as if it actually had been.

And even more, much more, than this: whole countries and continents repeat each other's mistakes after a while; it can happen even now, in an age when, it would seem, everything is clearly visible and obvious! No indeed: what some peoples have already suffered, considered, and rejected suddenly turns up among others as the last and newest word.

And here, too, the one and only substitute for experience we have not ourselves had is art, literature. We have been given a miraculous faculty: to be able to communicate despite differences in languages, customs, and social structures the life-experience of one whole nation to another whole nation—to communicate a difficult national experience many decades long which the second nation has never experienced at all. And in the most favorable case this may save a whole nation from a path which is unnecessary, or mistaken, or even fatal. And in this way the twistings and windings of human history are lessened.

I wish today from this Nobel Lecture platform to call insistent attention to this great and blessed faculty of art.

There is one other invaluable way in which literature communicates irrefutable and condensed human experience—from generation to generation. In this way it becomes the living memory of nations. In this way it keeps warm and preserves within itself its lost history in a way not subject to distortion and falsification. Thus literature, along with language, preserves the national soul.

(In recent times there has been much talk of the leveling of nations, of the disappearance of peoples in the caldron or contemporary civilization. I do agree with this, but discussion of this point is a separate matter. At this juncture it is merely appropriate to say that the disappearance of nationalities would impoverish us no less than if all people were to become identical, to possess one single, identical personality, one identical face. Nationalities are the wealth of humanity; they are its crystallized personalities; even the smallest among them has its own special coloration, hides within itself a particular facet of God's design.)

But woe to that nationality whose literature is cut short by forcible interference. This is no mere simple violation of "freedom of the press." This is a closing, a locking up, of the national heart, amputation of the national memory. That nationality has no memory of its own self. It is deprived of its spiritual unity. And even though compatriots apparently speak the same language, they suddenly cease to understand one another. Whole speechless generations are born and die off who do not tell each other about themselves, nor speak about themselves to their descendants. If such literary geniuses

6

AT VARIOUS TIMES and in various countries there have been heated, angry, and sophisticated arguments as to whether art and the artist may exist for their own sakes or whether they are required always to keep in mind their debt to society and to serve it, even though in an unbiased way. My own view on this is clear enough, but I am not here going to go into the lines of this argument again. One of the most brilliant statements on this theme was the Nobel Lecture of Albert Camus—and I can happily support its reasoning. Yes, and Russian literature has followed this direction for whole decades: not to let itself get lost in self-admiration, not to flit about too carelessly. I am not ashamed of this tradition and shall continue it myself as best I can. The concept has long been deeply rooted in Russian literature that a writer can do much for his people —and must.

We are not going to flout the RIGHT of the artist to express exclusively his own personal experiences and observations while at the same time paying little heed to everything going on in the rest of the world. We are not going to make a DEMAND on the artist in this respect; instead, we will reproach him, ask him, appeal to him, and coax him, for this is allowed us. Usually, after all, he develops his talent on his own only in part; he is endowed with most of it, ready-made, at birth, and along with his talent goes the responsibility for his free will. Let us grant that the artist OWES nobody anything; it is still painful to see how he CAN, by retreating into a world of his own creation or into the open spaces of subjective caprice, leave the real world in the hands of mercenary people who are often totally insignificant as well, and sometimes even out of their minds.

Our twentieth century has turned out to be crueler than those that went before it, nor did everything horrible in it end with its first half. Those same caveman emotions—greed, envy, unrestraint, mutual hatred—which, as they moved, assumed such high-sounding pseudonyms as class, race, mass, or trade-union struggle, are tearing our world apart and reducing it to chaos. Caveman unwillingness to accept compromises has been elevated into a theoretical principle and is considered to be a virtue of orthodoxy. It requires millions of victims in endless civil wars. It keeps drumming into our hearts that there are no stable and universal concepts of justice and good, that all values are fluid, that they change, and that this means one must always act as suits one's party. Any professional group, as soon as it finds a convenient moment TO GRAB SOMETHING OFF, even if it has not been earned, even if it is unneeded, will right away grab it off, and society can go fall apart. The upward and downward oscillations of Western society, as seen from outside, are approaching at both extremes that point where the entire system will be unable to return to a state of stability and must fall into ruin. Violence, continually less restrained by the confines of a legality established over the course of many generations, strides brazenly and victoriously through the whole world, unconcerned with the fact that its sterility has already been manifested and proven many times in history.

savage oppressors and rulers, and then we who take over from them, having put aside our grenades and submachine guns, will be just and sensitive." Don't you believe it! And those who have lived their lives and who understand—many of them at any rate—those who are able, if they wish, to refute the young DO NOT DARE to refute them, but even flatter them and fawn upon them, will do anything so as not to seem to be "conservatives"—and this again is a phenomenon of the Russian nineteenth century. Dostoyevsky called it "ENSLAVEMENT TO PROGRESSIVE FADS."

The spirit of Munich has by no means retreated into the past. It was not a brief episode. I would even be so bold as to say that the spirit of Munich dominates the twentieth century. The frightened civilized world found nothing better than concessions and smiles to counterpose to the sudden renewed assault of bare-fanged barbarism. The spirit of Munich is an illness of the will of prosperous people. It is the daily state of those who have given themselves over to their thirst for well-being at no matter what cost, to material prosperity as the principal goal of life on earth. Such people—and there are a multitude of them in the world of today

—choose passivity and retreat, anything so that their accustomed life should continue undisturbed, anything so as not to have to cross over into hardship today, while tomorrow, they hope, will take care of itself. (But tomorrow never will take care of itself! The retribution for cowardice will merely be all the more cruel. Courage and overcoming are given us only when we are willing to accept sacrifices.)

And we are also threatened by destruction because the physically compressed and crowded world is not being permitted to fuse spiritually, because the molecules of knowledge and sympathy are not allowed to leap freely from one half into the other. This is the ferocious danger of the BLOCKAGE OF INFORMATION FLOW between areas of the planet. Contemporary science knows that blockage of information flow leads to entropy, disintegration, and universal destruction. Blockage of information flow renders illusory those signatures on international agreements and treaties: within a SOUNDPROOFED and silenced zone any treaty whatsoever can be reinterpreted at will—or, better still, just forgotten. It is as if it had never existed. (This is something Orwell understood very well.) Within the soundproofed zone the inhabitants are not so much people of the Earth as they are like a Martian expeditionary force. They know nothing important about the rest of the Earth, and they are quite ready to march out and trample it in the sacred conviction that they are "liberating" it.

A quarter-century ago the United Nations Organization was born amid the high hopes of humanity. But, alas, in a world without morality it, too, was born without morality. It is not a United Nations Organization but a United Governments Organization, in which governments freely elected are equated with those which have imposed themselves by force, which seized power by force of arms. With self-seeking partiality, the majority in the UN concerns itself jealously with the freedom of certain peoples and carelessly neglects the freedom of others. By an obsequious vote it has rejected consideration of PRIVATE COMPLAINTS—the groans, the cries, and the prayers of isolated little people who are MERELY PEOPLE. For they are insects only, too small for such a great organization. The UN has never tried to make OBLIGATORY for governments AS A CONDITION of their membership the best document of its twenty-five years—the Declaration of

Human Rights—and thus it has consigned the little people to the will of governments they did not elect.

It might seem as if the whole face of the contemporary world is determined by scientists. All the technical steps of society are decided by them. It might seem as if the direction the world will take must depend, in fact, on the world-wide collaboration of scientists, not politicians—particularly when the example of a few individuals shows how much all of them could achieve together. But no, scientists have never made a clear attempt to become an important independent motive-force for humanity. Whole congresses back away from the sufferings of others: it is much cozier to stay within the bounds of science itself. That very same spirit of Munich has unfolded its enfeebling wings over them, too.

What, then, in this cruel, dynamic, explosive world, which stands at the very edge of its ten dooms, are the place and the role of the writer? We writers do not shoot off any rockets. We do not even push along the lowliest of hand carts. We are held in contempt by those who respect only material might. Is it not natural for us also to retreat, to lose our faith in the inviolability of good, in the indivisibility of truth, and merely impart to the world from the sidelines our bitter observations on how hopelessly humanity is corrupted, how degenerate people have become, and how hard it is for delicate and beautiful souls to live among them?

But even this escape does not exist for us. Once having taken up THE WORD, it is never again possible to turn away. The writer is no sideline judge of his compatriots and contemporaries. He is guilty along with them of all the evil committed in his native land or by his people. And if the tanks of his fatherland have shed blood on the asphalt of a foreign capital, the brown stains have for all eternity spattered the writer's face. And if on a fateful night a sleeping, trusting friend has been choked to death, there are black and blue marks from the rope on the writer's palms. And if the young fellow citizens of his country impudently proclaim the superiority of debauchery to modest labor, or go in for narcotics, or seize HOSTAGES—then all of this evil stink mingles in the breath of the writer.

Shall we find within us the insolence to declare that we are not responsible for the ulcers of today's world?

7

However, I am encouraged and emboldened by the vital perception of WORLD LITERATURE as the one great heart which beats for the concerns and misfortunes of our world, even though these are represented and visible in different, separate ways in each of its corners.

Beyond the age-old national literatures there existed from early times the concept of world literature—viewed as a network of connecting lines joining the peaks of national literatures, and as the totality of reciprocal literary influences. But there used to be a time lag: readers and writers learned of writers in other languages only after delays that were sometimes ages long, so that mutual influences were also delayed, and world literature as a network of connecting lines joining national literary peaks

Norwegian writers and artists hospitably readied a shelter for me in the event of the expulsion from my motherland which threatened me. And then, in the end, my nomination for the Nobel Prize itself was initiated, not in the country in which I live and write, but by François Mauriac and his colleagues. More than this, national writers' organizations expressed their unanimous support of me.

And this was how I perceived and felt in my own case that world literature was not an abstraction, not something which had not yet crystallized, something created by the scholars of literature, but was a certain common body and common spirit, a living unity of the heart, in which the growing spiritual unity of humanity was expressed. And state boundaries are still being reddened by blood and heated by high-tension wires and by bursts of fire from automatic weapons, and certain ministries of internal affairs still imagine that literature, too, is an "internal affair" of the countries at their disposal, and newspaper headlines still read: "They do not have the right to interfere in our internal affairs!" Meanwhile there is no such thing left on our Earth as INTERNAL AFFAIRS. And the only salvation of humanity lies in everyone concerning himself with everything everywhere: the peoples of the East would then not be totally indifferent to what takes place in the West; and the peoples of the West would not be totally indifferent to what takes place in the East. Literature, one of the most delicate and responsive instruments of human existence, has been the first to take hold of, to assimilate, to seize upon this feeling of the growing unity of humanity. And so, today, I am appealing to world literature with conviction—to hundreds of friends whom I have never met face to face and whom I perhaps never will see.

Friends! If we are worth anything, let us try to help! In our own countries, torn asunder by the discord of parties, movements, castes, and groups, who is it who has from the earliest ages been a force not for disunity but for unity? This in essence is the position of writers: the spokesmen for their national language—the principal tie binding together a nation, binding together the very Earth occupied by a people, and in fortunate cases their national soul also.

I think that world literature has it within its power in these frightening hours to help humanity know itself truly despite what prejudiced people and parties are attempting to instill; to communicate the condensed experience of one region to another in such a way that we will cease to be split apart and our eyes will no longer be dazzled, the units of measurement on our scales of values will correspond to one another, and some peoples may come to know the true history of others accurately and concisely and with that perception and pain they would feel if they had experienced it themselves—and thus be protected from repeating the same errors. And at the same time we ourselves can perhaps develop within ourselves a WORLD VIEW: seeing with the center of the eye, like every human being, what is close, and with the edge of the eye registering what is happening in the rest of the world. And so we can bring world-wide standards into correlation and adhere to them.

And who, if not the writers, are to express condemnation not only of their own bankrupt rulers (and in some countries this is the easiest way of all to earn a living and everyone except those who are too lazy is occupied with it) but also of their own society, whether it be a matter of its craven humiliation or its complacent weakness, or the featherbrained escapades of youth, or young pirates brandishing knives?

People will ask what literature can do in the face of the pitiless assault of open violence? Well, let us not forget that violence does not have its own separate existence and is, in fact, incapable of having it: it is invariably interwoven with THE LIE. They have the closest of kinship, the most profound natural tie: violence has nothing with which to cover itself except the lie, and the lie has nothing to stand on other than violence. Once someone has proclaimed violence as his METHOD, he must inexorably select the lie as his PRINCIPLE. At its birth violence acts openly and even takes pride in itself. But as soon as it is reinforced and its position is strengthened, it begins to sense the rarefied atmosphere around it, and it can go further only when fogged about with lies, cloaked in honeyed, hypocritical words. It does not always nor invariably choke its victims; more often it demands of them only the oath of the lie, only participation in the lie.

Simple is the ordinary courageous human being's act of not participating in the lie, of not supporting false actions! What his stand says is: "So be it that *this* takes place in the world, that it even reigns in the world—but let it not be with my complicity." Writers and artists have a greater opportunity: TO CONQUER THE LIE! In battle with the lie, art has always been victorious, always wins out, visibly, incontrovertibly for all! The lie can stand up and win out over much in the world—but not over art.

And as soon as the lie is dispersed, the repulsive nakedness of violence is exposed, and violence will collapse in impotence.

And that is why, my friends, I think that we are capable of helping the world in its white-hot hour of trial. We must not reconcile ourselves to being defenseless and disarmed; we must not sink into a heedless, feckless life—but go out to the field of battle.

In the Russian language there are some favorite proverbs on TRUTH. They express enduringly the immense folk experience, and are sometimes quite surprising:

"ONE WORD OF TRUTH OUTWEIGHS THE WHOLE WORLD."

And so it is that my own activity is founded on so apparently fantastic a violation of the law of the conservation of energy and mass, as is my appeal to the writers of the whole world.